Radical
Reptiles

Radical Reptiles

Sara Swan Miller

Watts LIBRARY

Franklin Watts
A Division of Grolier Publishing
New York • London • Hong Kong • Sydney
Danbury, Connecticut

Note to readers: Definitions for words in **bold** can be found in the Glossary at the back of this book.

Photographs ©: Animals Animals: 20 (Bill Beatty), 10 bottom (Michael Fogden), 22, 26 (Zig Leszczynski), 21 (Klaus Uhlenhut); BBC Natural History Unit: 30 (John Cancalosi), 23 (Pete Oxford), 9 top (Mike Pitts), 24, 25 (Premaphotos); Brian Kenney: 5 bottom, 12, 27, 45; NHPA: 36 (Anthony Bannister), 18 top (Martin Harvey), 10 top (Jean-Louis Le Moigne), 34 (Karl Switak); Peter Arnold Inc.: 33 (Fred Bruemmer), 6, 7 (Martha Cooper), 14, 42, 43 (R. Andrew Odum), 16 top (Hans Pfletschinger), 46 (Kevin Schafer), cover (Secret Sea Visions), 28, 29 (Roland Seitre), 5 top, 9 bottom (Michael Sewell); Visuals Unlimited: 40, 48 (Joe McDonald), 2 (Jim Merli), 18 bottom (Brian Rogers), 39 (Tom J. Ulrich), 16 bottom (William J. Weber).

The photograph on the cover shows a Komodo dragon. The photograph opposite the title page shows a Gila monster.

Visit Franklin Watts on the Internet at:
http://publishing.grolier.com

Library of Congress Cataloging-in-Publication Data

Miller, Sara Swan
    Radical Reptiles / by Sara Swan Miller
        p.   cm.— (Watts Library)
    Includes bibliographical references and index.
    Summary: Describes several species of reptiles that have unusual appearances, habitats, or behaviors.
    ISBN 0-531-11794-4 (lib. bdg.)   0-531-13989-1 (pbk.)
    1. Reptiles—Juvenile literature. [1. Reptiles.] I. Title. II. Series.
QL644.2. M53 2000
597.9—dc21   99-057020

Contents

*Alligators
are reptiles.*

Chapter One

What Is a Reptile?

Do you know what a reptile is? You probably know that snakes are reptiles. So are lizards and turtles—but frogs aren't reptiles, and neither are fish. So what's the difference? Scientists organize plants and animals into categories according to specific differences and similarities. If you've learned about reptiles in school, you may know some of the traits that make them different from animals in other groups.

Reptiles are a group of animals that include turtles, lizards, snakes, tuataras, alligators, and crocodiles. They are **cold-blooded**. That means a reptile's body temperature stays about the same as the temperature of its surroundings. Reptiles need to stay warm in order to move about. They warm up in the sun, and cool off in the shade. Since reptiles are unable to regulate their own body temperature like birds or mammals, most of them live in warm places. Reptiles are **vertebrates**—animals that have backbones.

Most reptiles have dry, scaly skin. Because their eggs are protected by a tough, leathery shell, reptile eggs don't dry out. That's why reptiles can lay eggs on land. Turtles are protected by a bony shell that is covered with horny plates and grows out of their backbone. Lizards have four legs and a tail, and they can run around on land. Sleek, tight-skinned snakes have no legs, but they slither along the ground with the help of their strong muscles. Tuataras look a lot like lizards, but they don't have ear holes. Crocodiles and alligators are armored reptiles

Everything in Its Place

All living things can be organized into categories depending on their characteristics. Plants and animals are in two of the highest categories called **kingdoms**. Those top-level categories are broken up into many subcategories, with each category having more in common than the one before. Reptiles make up one **class** of living things, a middle level category. Insects, amphibians, mammals, and birds are also classes of animals. The science of organizing living things into these groups is called **taxonomy**.

that live mostly in the water. They usually move slowly and heavily when they're on land—but they can move surprisingly quickly if they need to!

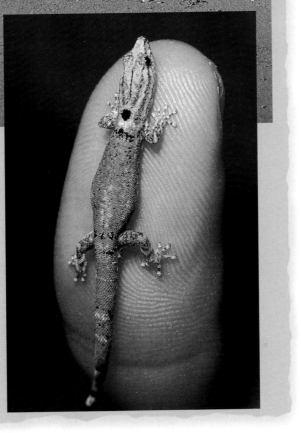

Giant Lizards, Tiny Lizards

The huge Komodo dragon grows up to 10 feet (3 meters) long. The monitor gecko is smaller than your smallest finger.

Giant Snakes, Tiny Snakes

Anacondas can grow up to 33 feet (10 m) long. The tiny threadsnake is less than 6 inches (15 centimeters) long.

If you said all that when describing a reptile, you'd be right—up to a point. Those are some of the basic "rules" that describe how reptiles are different from amphibians, birds, mammals, and other classes of animals. Some reptiles don't look the way they're "supposed" to look, or behave the way we expect them to behave. The world of reptiles is full of surprises!

Blue chameleons look different from other lizards.

Chapter Two

Strange Shapes and Colors

You probably think you know what a lizard looks like—a slim, scaly reptile with four legs and a long tail. If you picture a snake, you probably imagine a long, sleek, legless creature slithering along the ground. Usually you'd be right. Most lizards and snakes do fit these descriptions, but not all of them. Over millions of years, many different animals have **evolved**, or developed special adaptations, to help them survive in their environments. Sometimes, those evolutionary changes result in animals with strange behaviors and strange looks—and reptiles are no exception. Some reptiles just don't look the way you'd expect a reptile to look.

Glass Lizards

You might not consider the glass lizard to be a lizard, because it has no legs! If you saw a glass lizard slithering through the grass in the eastern United States, you might think it was a striped snake.

How do scientists tell the difference between a lizard and a snake? First, a lizard has ear openings on the sides of its head,

This slender glass lizard looks like a snake.

but a snake has no ear holes. Also, a lizard can open and close its eyelids, but a snake cannot do this. Scientists also look at a reptile's skeleton, particularly the bones in its head, to tell what kind of reptile it is. A lizard's skull is constructed in a way that lets it turn its head very easily. It also has special jawbones that lift its snout up when it eats. Since the glass lizard fits this description, it's a lizard—even without legs.

A glass lizard has bony plates in its skin that act like armor. These plates protect it from enemies, but they also make its body so stiff that it would have a lot of trouble breathing without a special adaptation. Running down both sides of its body, the glass lizard has a groove of soft scales. Those grooves let its body expand enough to fill its lungs with air.

Although glass lizards are as shiny as glass, that isn't what gives them their name. The glass lizard has an unusual defense against predators. When an enemy grabs a glass lizard's tail, the tail shatters to bits. The confused predator is left holding nothing but little, twitching pieces of tail, and the lizard gets away. The lucky glass lizard soon grows another tail and can trick another enemy.

Worm Lizards

If you see a bird pulling what looks like a worm out of the ground, look again. It may look like a worm, and wiggle like a worm, but it might actually be another kind of legless lizard. Unless something pulls the legless worm lizard of South America out of the ground, you may never see one. The worm

Leaping Lizards!

One Australian legless lizard can leap straight into the air. Strong tail muscles allow it to shoot up like a wriggling spring.

The slowworm is really a lizard.

A worm lizard is a great underground burrower.

lizard spends most of its life underground, burrowing under the soil in search of insects and worms to eat.

The worm lizard is well adapted for an underground life. Its snout is blunt, and its mouth is under its chin, so it can burrow easily. Its scales aren't like other reptile scales, either. Instead of having neat rows of scales down its back, the worm lizard's scales form rings around its slim body. That arrangement helps it wriggle through the soil like a worm.

Some scientists don't count worm lizards as lizards; they place them in a group of their own. Lizards and snakes have a left lung that is smaller than the right lung, but in the worm lizards, the right lung is smaller. Some worm lizards don't even have a right lung. Also, their skull bones are different, and the hatching young have an **egg tooth** used to pierce the eggshell. Finally, unlike other lizards, they have no ear openings, and their eyes are covered with skin. Lizards or not, these reptiles are certainly very strange!

Because it can barely see and has no ears, the worm lizard has developed a special way to hunt for food. It has a unique way of detecting sounds. Bones in the worm lizard's throat connect with plates on each side of its jaw, and scales on its jaw act as a sort of eardrum. So a worm lizard, earless though it is, can hear quite well!

Thorny Devils

The thorny devil of Australia may be the strangest-looking lizard you'll ever see. It's covered with horns, warts, knobs, and armored scales—and it really does look hideous! This lizard, *Moloch horridus*, gets its first name from a fierce, bloodthirsty god named Moloch, and its second name means "dreadful." This ghastly name and horrid appearance really doesn't fit the personality of the thorny devil. It is actually a perfectly gentle creature, and it never grows more than 8 inches (20 cm) long.

A thorny devil can look quite scary.

Enemies may mistake the tough knob on top for a thorny devil's head.

The thorny devil uses its spikes and knobs to protect itself from predators, including large birds, big lizards, and dingoes, or wild dogs. It has other ways of protecting itself too. It has a secret weapon on the back of its neck—an odd-looking knob. When a thorny devil feels threatened, it tucks its head down between its forelegs. The knob then sticks up in the air. Any enemy that tried to attack this decoy "head" would find itself gnawing at a hard knob. The thorny devil can also puff itself up with air when it's attacked, which makes it look too big to swallow.

When it is warm or actively feeding, the thorny devil is pale yellow or red. But when it feels cold or scared, it turns a dark olive color. These colors help keep the lizard safe from enemies. It walks slowly, and often freezes in place—another good way to escape unwanted attention.

The spikes on a thorny devil's head have another use besides defense. It lives in the desert, where there is little rain. But drops of dew condense on its spikes and then run down grooves to the corners of its mouth. That's all the water a thorny devil needs.

Wormsnakes

After learning about legless lizards, snakes with something like legs shouldn't be too much of a surprise. Snakes don't have real legs, but the wormsnakes of Australia come close. These primitive snakes still have traces of bones in their **pelvis** where legs would be attached. That leads scientists to believe that, once upon a time, wormsnakes probably had legs. Over many years, though, they evolved so that just a hint of those legs remains.

It's easy to guess how wormsnakes got their name. They are long and slender, and look a lot like worms. They have no eyes, just small, dark spots on their heads. They can tell the difference between light and dark, but that's about all.

A Strange Relative

The horned toad is actually not a toad—it's a lizard, and a cousin of the thorny devil. When it's scared, it can spurt blood from the corners of its eyes to startle enemies.

Like worms, worm-snakes have no eyes.

Wormsnakes don't really need eyes though. They spend their lives burrowing along underground, sniffling out worms and insect eggs.

One of the strangest wormsnakes is the tiny flowerpot snake. All flowerpot snakes are females! Are you wondering how they mate? The answer is they don't need to. Females give birth to daughters, who give birth to daughters, who give birth to daughters. This odd way of reproducing without a male is called **parthenogenesis** (par-thuh-noh-JEN-uh-sis). A few other animals, including walking sticks, aphids, fruit-flies, and the aquarium fish called mollies can also reproduce this way.

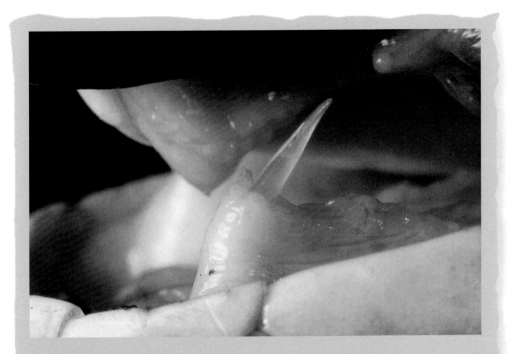

Beware!

Wormsnakes aren't **venomous**, but many other snakes are. The inland taipan of Australia is the world's most poisonous snake. The venom in a single bite could kill 250,000 mice!

Most lizards are not poiso-nous. Only the Gila monster of the southwestern United States has venom, and it is not a terribly strong poison. If you were bitten by a gila monster, the bite would hurt and swell, but it couldn't kill you.

You might think that without mating, flowerpot snakes would be unable to adapt to changing conditions and would become extinct. So far, however, they have been very success-ful and have spread all around the world. Because these tiny snakes can hide in small containers of soil such as flowerpots, people have unknowingly carried the flowerpot snakes along to all kinds of new places.

Elephant's Trunk Snakes

The snakes you are familiar with are probably all slim and muscular with tight-fitting skin. Can you picture a snake with baggy skin? The aptly named elephant's trunk snake of Asia has skin that flops around its body!

An elephant's trunk snake is a type of file snake. Like other file snakes, it spends its life underwater. It has trouble moving on land, but when it swims, its baggy skin flattens out and acts like a big paddle that moves the snake swiftly along.

Like other file snakes, an elephant's trunk snake has distinctive skin. It's covered with small, conical scales that look like the surface of a nail file. That rough skin is a good adaptation. Like pythons, the file snake squeezes its prey to kill it. File snakes prey on slippery fish, and the snake's rough skin helps them hold onto their prey, no matter how slippery.

The baggy elephant's trunk snake is clumsy on land.

Frog or Lizard?

Most lizards use their jaws and teeth to catch their prey—but not the chameleon. It uses its sharp eyes and its long, sticky tongue. The chameleon hides in ambush, waiting for an insect to fly by. It can turn its eyes in different directions at the same time. When an unsuspecting fly comes by, the chameleon's excellent eyesight helps it take aim. One quick lick, and that fly is lunch!

Most lizards have separate toes, so they can run swiftly. The toes of the Namib web-footed gecko, however, are webbed like a frog's. It doesn't use its webbed feet for swimming. This lizard lives in the Namib Desert in Africa, where there is no water in sight. It uses its webbed feet to dig burrows in the sand, where it can rest in the blazing heat of day. Now that's a useful adaptation!

*A male flying dragon
spreads his "wings."*

Chapter Three

Can Reptiles Fly?

Look up in the sky—it's a bird! It's a plane! It's a *reptile*? If you were looking for snakes and lizards, you might try to find them scampering or slithering along the ground. You might look for water snakes in a pond, a stream, or the ocean. You might even look in the trees for snakes and lizards hiding in the branches. You probably wouldn't expect to see a lizard or snake flying through the air. Believe it or not, though, some kinds of reptiles do!

Flying Dragons

The flying dragon is a lizard that lives in Southeast Asia. It is specially adapted to glide from tree to tree. Five to seven of its long ribs have folds of skin that stretch between them. To take off, the flying dragon pulls its ribs forward and stretches out the folds of skin to form colorful "wings." It doesn't actually flap its wings and fly like a bird, but it can glide up to 195 feet (60 m) from tree to tree. With small movements of its wings and tail, the lizard can control its direction and speed very precisely.

Gliding off to another tree is a great way to escape from a predator. When the lizard lands at its destination, it's wings close up, and the animal blends perfectly with its leafy surroundings.

It's hard to imagine why people call these lizards flying *dragons*, though. One of these tiny lizards is small enough to fit in the palm of your hand.

A Malayan Flying Dragon ready to take off.

A gliding gecko's feet are good for both gliding and gripping.

Gliding Geckos

The gliding gecko of Southeast Asia is more of a parachute jumper than a hang glider. This odd-looking gecko has a flat body with large folds of skin along its head, sides, and tail. When an enemy attacks it, the gecko can hurl itself from a tree and glide down to a safe place. It simply spreads its legs and tail wide, stretches out its skin flaps, and floats to a lower branch.

Gliding geckos spend all their lives in the trees, so maybe it is no surprise that they have learned to glide out of harm's way. They blend well with their surroundings. Their greenish-blue coloring makes them look like a lichen-covered branch.

These lizards are well suited to life in the trees. Their toe pads are covered with microscopic "hooks" that help them cling to tree branches. Those toes can grab onto almost any surface. Geckos can run across a ceiling, and even climb up a pane of glass!

Unlike most lizards, geckos have no eyelids. Instead, their eyes are covered with transparent scales, called "spectacles." When their spectacles get dirty, geckos just lick them clean.

Most lizards feed during the day, when the sun can warm them up. But gliding geckos and many other geckos rest during the day and hunt all night long. They catch insects and spiders at night that daytime lizards miss.

Flying Snakes

Surprisingly, some snakes fly from tree to tree instead of just dropping to the ground. The flying snakes of Asia are specially adapted for gliding through the air. When a flying snake is coiled around a branch, its body is round. But when it launches itself into the air, it spreads out its ribs, making its body broad, flat, and concave like the inside of a bowl. Because of its special shape, a flying snake can swoop slowly down to another tree.

Other snakes sometimes dive out of trees, but flying snakes are the only ones built especially for gliding. Bushsnakes and parrotsnakes have to wiggle their way through the air and hope for the best.

Flying is a fast way to escape from big birds or larger snakes. It's also a good way to catch the skinks that flying snakes like to eat. Skinks are fast, slippery lizards, but flying snakes have jaws that are specially adapted to grip a wriggling skink. Another snake in the same family, the wolfsnake, uses its large front teeth to catch slippery skinks.

A flying snake ready to launch.

Most reptiles, like this India python, hatch from eggs.

Chapter Four

Do All Reptiles Lay Eggs?

Perhaps you know how most reptiles reproduce. Each spring, after mating, a female lays her leathery-shelled eggs in a burrow she has made. She covers them up, and then leaves them to hatch on their own. The eggs are warmed by the sun and the soil or sand around them. That is true of most reptiles, but, as you have probably guessed, some reptiles have a different way of doing things. In fact, some reptiles don't even lay eggs!

Why Lay Eggs?

Several kinds of snakes and lizards give birth to live young instead of laying eggs. Although a reptile isn't warm-blooded, a mother reptile who carries her young inside her body can keep them warm by basking in the sun and finding warm places to nest. Some pregnant females spend most of their time sunning themselves. The heat speeds up the development of the young so that they are born early enough in the year to grow big and get ready for winter.

Bearing live young has some disadvantages too. A pregnant mother is slowed down by a heavy burden of young, and can easily fall prey to predators. Also, she usually doesn't eat until the young are born, and she may die of starvation soon after giving birth. Reptiles that lay eggs don't have those problems, so most reptiles that live in warm places lay eggs. The sun warms the eggs, and the mother goes off on her own.

Garter Snakes

Garter snakes are so common and ordinary looking that you would never suspect that they are at all strange—but they are. Garter snakes don't lay eggs, but give birth to live young. Garter snakes are also one of the few snakes that can survive in very cold places. The red-sided garter snake, for instance, lives in the north of Canada. When the harsh winter comes, garter snakes hibernate, gathering together in huge groups in rock crevices. They hibernate in places below the frost line, where it is a little warmer.

When hundreds of garter snakes all come out of their burrows in the spring, it is an amazing sight. Mating comes soon after they emerge from their winter homes. The females give off a chemical substance called a **pheromone** (FER-uh-mohn), which has an odor that tells the males when the females are ready to mate. Sometimes, one female is surrounded by a writhing ball of interested males.

Usually, the first male to reach the female mates with her. Sometimes, however, a male uses a special trick. He gives off a scent that smells like a female pheromone, which confuses the other males. The tricky male knows which snake is the real female, however. He heads right for her and mates while the other snakes are still trying to figure out who's who.

This tangle of redsided garter snakes contains a female ready to mate.

33

Other Eggless Snakes

Since file snakes, including the elephant's trunk snakes, live in the water, they can't lay eggs. They have live young, too.

Inside the mother's body, each baby snake gets food from a **yolk sac**. It is also wrapped in a membrane called a **chorion**, which provides oxygen. About 3 months after the parents mate, the young come wriggling out of the female. In about 2 years they are ready to give birth to their own young.

Puff Adders

The poisonous puff adders of Africa don't lay eggs either. Like garter snakes, they give birth to live young. When the males come out of hibernation in the spring, they are drab-looking like the females. Soon after emerging, they shed their old skin. Their new skin is brightly colored, which helps the males to attract a mate.

This puff adder has just shed its skin.

Sometimes two males are interested in the same female. First, they check out each other's size. If one puff adder is a lot

smaller, it quickly slithers away. If they are about the same size, though, they fight over the female. They don't bite each other, because the venom of a puff adder is so poisonous that both of them might die. Instead, they wrestle until one gives up.

The female carries the developing young inside her body for about two months. She spends most of her time basking in the sun, and the **embryos** develop quickly. All that time the mother doesn't eat. By the time the twenty to eighty young she carries are strong enough to fend for themselves, the female is skinny and starving. Many females die after they give birth. Those that survive spend much of their time eating, and most can't store enough energy to be able to mate again until the following year. As a result, most female puff adders usually give birth only once every 2 or 3 years.

When a puff adder is attacked, it puffs up its body with air and exhales loud hisses and puffs. Then it strikes! Puff adders are among the most venomous snakes in the world. They can inject three times the venom needed to kill an adult person. Because they blend well with their surroundings, they are easy to step on. Believe it or not, these deadly snakes have enemies. Snake-eagles catch and eat them, poison and all!

Armadillo Girdle-Tailed Lizards

Usually, reptiles that live in warm places lay eggs, while reptiles that live in cold places bear live young. They can make sure their embryos stay warm by basking in the sun. But again, some reptiles are different. For example, the armadillo girdle-tailed lizards live in warm parts of Africa, but the female carries her young inside her body until they are born. She bears between one and six young that have been well nourished by their yolk sacs. By the time they are born, they are ready to take care of themselves, and many of them survive and live to adulthood. It takes a while for them to be ready to bear young themselves, but they can live to be quite old. An armadillo girdle-tailed lizard has been known to live for 25 years in captivity.

It's hard to know why a lizard that lives in such a warm part of the world bears live young. However, if the female laid only six eggs, it's possible that none of them would survive. Many predators like to eat reptile eggs, so it makes sense that the armadillo girdle-tailed lizard has adapted to bearing live offspring to protect its small batches of young.

An armadillo girdle-tailed lizard curls up to protect itself.

An armadillo girdle-tailed lizard has an odd appearance. It has large, prickly scales that grow in rings around its body and tail. Those spines help it defend itself from enemies. They also help it wedge itself tightly into rock crevices for safety.

This lizard has another good defense. When it's scared, it can roll up and grip its tail in its mouth. It curls into a ring with scaly armor on the outside protecting its soft belly inside. Although it can't roll away, it's safe from the jaws of many hungry predators.

Brazilian Skinks

A Brazilian skink may look like any ordinary lizard, but the way it bears its young is completely different. A few other lizards bear live young, but the embryos live off nourishment from a yolk sac. A mother Brazilian skink actually has a **placenta**, like mammals—including humans.

A placenta is full of blood vessels that carry nutrients and oxygen to the embryo. The female Brazilian skink is the only lizard that nourishes the embryo through her own body. In the beginning, the embryo is too tiny to see. By the time it is ready to be born, however, it has grown 38,000 times bigger. The placenta is clearly a good way of nourishing offspring.

Skinks are covered with smooth, overlapping scales, like fish. Skinks spend their time on land or underground in burrows. Some skinks are called "sandfish." Those smooth scales keep mud from sticking to their bodies.

The Tuatara

The tuatara lays eggs, but only once in 4 years! In between, the female tuatara builds up her strength by eating as many insects and other small creatures as she can find. Once a tuatara lays her eggs, it may take up to 15 months before they hatch. That's the longest **incubation period** of any reptile.

Tuataras mate in the late summer. The male tuatara stakes out a territory and starts "showing off" for the females. He inflates his body, raises the crests that run down his back, and lifts his spines. This display attracts the females and warns other males to stay away!

If another male comes into a male's territory, the two may have a showdown. They stand near each other, then slowly open their mouths wide and quickly snap them shut. If that doesn't scare one of them away, the two males get into a fight. They wrestle on the ground, thrashing and croaking. The loser often goes away with bloody wounds or broken bones.

The female digs a burrow and lays up to 19 eggs in it. Then she spends several nights filling up the burrow with soil. Even after she has buried the eggs, she stays near the nest for several nights, guarding the nest. Other females may try to dig up the nest and lay their own eggs in it, and the female will fight fiercely if anyone tries. Tuataras are one of the few reptiles that defend their nests.

Scientists believe that tuataras lived all over the world from 225 million to 120 million years ago—long before the dinosaurs. Now they are found only on islands around New Zealand. Although they look like lizards, scientists classify them in their own **order**—the Rhynchocephalia (rin-koh-suh-FAYL-yuh), which means "beak-headed." Unlike lizards, tuataras have no ear openings, and they have hooks on the end of some of their ribs, like birds.

Tuataras also have a strange "third eye" on the top of their head. It has a lens and a retina and is connected by nerves to the tuatara's brain. The third eye is sensitive to sunlight and tells the tuatara when it has had too much sun or not enough. It helps a tuatara stay at the right temperature.

Tuataras spend a lot of time resting.

39

*Everyone likes
box turtles!*

Chapter Five

Strange Turtles

Of course you know what a turtle looks like. It lives inside a hard, bony shell. The top part of the shell, called the **carapace**, protects the turtle's back, and the bottom part, the **plastron**, protects its belly. Both the plastron and the carapace are covered with horny scales, or **scutes**. The carapace is joined to the backbone and ribs, so that they are part of the shell. When a turtle feels threatened, it pulls its head and legs into its hard, safe shell.

Like other reptiles, turtles need to be warm in order to move about. During cold weather, they hibernate until the sun can warm them again. That's why you won't find turtles in the far north.

Some turtles, however, aren't quite what you would expect. Some look very strange. Others seem to have the wrong kind of shell. Even turtles break the rules sometimes!

Matamatas

The matamata of the South American rain forests may be the strangest-looking turtle of all. It is very well camouflaged—it looks like a pile of rubbish lying on the riverbed. The ridges on its flat shell make it look like a piece of bark. Along its head and neck are flaps of skin, which look like weeds or fallen leaves swaying in the current. Top all that off with **algae** growing from its carapace, and you get a creature perfectly disguised as a bunch of weeds, decaying leaves, and sticks.

The matamata lies motionless on the riverbed, and waits patiently for its prey. The only time it moves is when it needs to breathe. Then it stretches up its long snake-like neck to take a breath of air from the surface. When a fish swims too close to the matamata, it stretches out its

Alligator Snapping Turtle

The strange-looking alligator snapper has a wiggling pink "worm" on its tongue. If a fish tries to eat the worm, the snapper has a fish dinner!

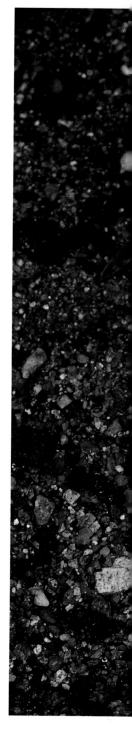

42

A matamata is an odd-looking turtle.

neck and opens its big mouth. Then it sucks in a big mouthful of water—and sometimes, nearby fish too! The water drains out, and the matamata has fish for dinner.

Most turtles have sharp, horny edges on their jaws, but not the matamata. It has soft, fleshy jaws, which are no good for snapping up fish. It doesn't need horny jaws, because it sucks up its prey like a vacuum cleaner.

The matamata has a few other quirks too. It has tiny eyes placed in front of its mouth, a snout like a small elephant's trunk, and a V-shaped mouth tucked underneath. Face to face, a matamata looks as though it's grinning. Its small eyes aren't much good at seeing prey. Instead, it depends on its ears to pick up vibrations in the water.

Soft-Shelled Turtles

Believe it or not, some turtles don't have hard shells. A soft-shelled turtle isn't covered with horny scales, and it doesn't even have bone under the edges of its shell. Instead, it has a flexible shell covered by a tough, leathery skin. It looks sort of like a dish with a head, legs, and a tail.

However it looks, a soft-shelled turtle is well adapted to life in North American streams and lakes. Its smooth skin and the flexible edges of its shell help it to swim swiftly through open water. It spends much of its time hiding on the bottom. It can dig its flat body into the mud, and predators don't see it. If it is attacked, a soft-shell can defend itself well with its razor-sharp, horny jaws.

Where Can You Find Them?

Soft-shell turtles live in rivers and lakes in North America, Africa, and Asia.

44

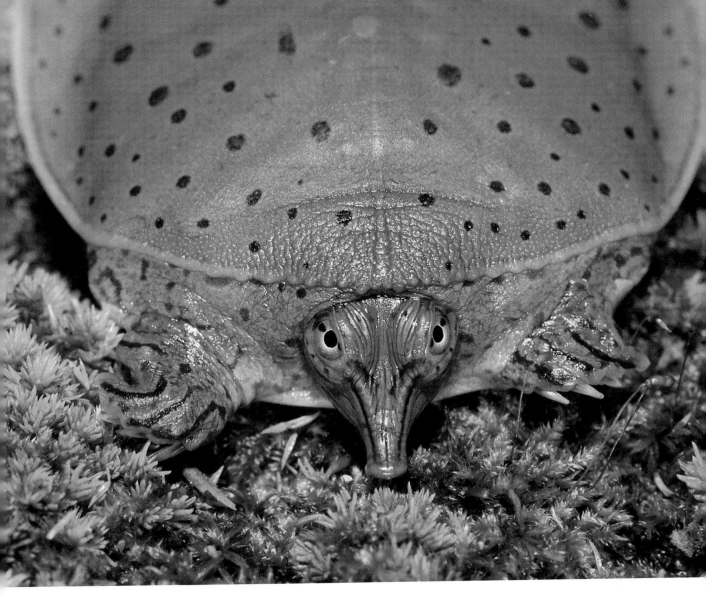

When a soft-shelled turtle needs to breathe, it stretches its long neck and snout up to the surface for air, leaving its body hidden in the mud. It can even breathe underwater if there's enough oxygen. The many blood vessels in its throat can absorb oxygen from the water, and it can also breathe underwater through its leathery skin. A soft-shell does quite well without a hard shell!

A spiny soft-shelled turtle heads for the safety of the pond.

Leatherback Turtles

A leatherback turtle doesn't have the usual kind of shell, either. Instead of horny scales, its shell is covered with a leathery skin. This turtle looks as though a big piece of black rubber has been stretched tightly over its body. The shell underneath is not made of thick bony plates like that of other turtles. It's just a thin layer of bone.

Leatherback turtles come out on land only to lay their eggs.

A leatherback is well adapted to life in the ocean. It uses its strong forelegs like paddles to propel its streamlined body. It's not weighed down by a heavy shell, so it travels at quite a clip. This marine turtle likes to feed on jellyfish, and is specially equipped to eat these slippery creatures. It has knife-sharp jaws with deep notches that can grip and easily slice up its prey. There are even spines inside its throat that keep jellyfish from slipping back out.

Unlike most turtles, leatherbacks can stand very cold temperatures. Every year, these turtles swim thousands of miles from the tropics, where they nest, all the way to the chilly waters off Newfoundland. A thick layer of oily fat under the leatherback's skin lets it hunt in water far too cold for any other turtle—so it has plenty of jellyfish all to itself.

Endangered!

Leatherbacks are becoming rare. One reason that they are endangered is that they sometimes eat plastic bags, thinking they are jellyfish. That can be fatal.

A sungazer lizard basks in the sun.

Chapter Six

Those Radical Reptiles

It's easier to make sense of the world around you if there are clear rules to follow and clear categories to put things in. When it comes to reptiles, however, there are so many exceptions to the standard "rules" that you might start wondering what the rules were in the first place.

Now that you know about some of the unusual reptiles in the world, you may have a different idea of what a reptile really is. Maybe the next time someone asks you what a reptile is, you'll have some different answers. You might say, "*Most* reptiles lay tough-shelled eggs," or "*Most* reptiles can't stand too much cold." You'd be right to say "*Almost all* turtles have hard, bony shells," and "*Most* lizards have four legs," and "*Most* snakes have tight, sleek skins."

Then, perhaps, you could go on to describe some of the reptiles that break all the rules. Reptiles certainly can be strange!

Radical Reptiles Around the World

Common name	Scientific name	Where found
Komodo dragon	*Varanus komodoensis*	Indonesian Islands
Monitor gecko	*Sphaerodactylus parthenopion*	British Virgin Islands, Cocos Island, Puerto Rico
Anaconda	*Eunectes* spp. (four species)	South America, east of the Andes
Threadsnake	*Leptotyphlops* spp.	Worldwide
Glass lizard	*Ophisaurus* spp.	Northeastern Mexico, southeastern and central USA, Eurasia
Thorny devil	*Moloch horridus*	Australia
Horned lizard or horned toad	*Phrynsoma* spp.	American southwest, Mexico
Flowerpot snakes	*Ramphotyphlops* spp.	Originally Southeast Asia, but now in Florida, Mexico, Hawaii too.
Wormsnake or blindsnake	*Ramphotyphlops nigrescens*	Australia
Inland taipan	*Oxyuranus microlepidotus*	Australia
Gila monster	*Heloderma suspectum*	Southwestern USA, Mexico
Elephant's trunk snake	*Acrochordus javanicus*	Southeast Asia, Australia, India, New Guinea
Namib web-footed gecko	*Palmatogecko rangei*	Africa south of Sahara Desert
Flying dragon	*Draco* spp.	Southeast Asia, East Indies, Philippines
Flying snakes	*Chrysopelea* spp.	Southeast and South Asia

continued next page

Radical Reptiles Around the World *continued*

Common name	Scientific name	Where found
Gliding gecko	*Ptychozoon* spp.	Southeast Asia
Red-sided garter snake	*Thamnophis siritalis parietalus*	Western USA and Canada
Puff adder	*Bitis arietans*	Africa and the Middle East
Armadillo girdle-tailed lizard	*Cordylus cataphractus*	South Africa
Brazilian skink	*Mabuya heathi*	South America
Tuatara	*Sphenodon* spp.	Islands off New Zealand coast
Matamata	*Chelus fimbriatus*	Northern South America
Alligator snapping turtle	*Macroclemys temminckii*	Southeastern United States
Spiny soft-shell turtles	*Apalone* spp.	Rivers and lakes in North America, Africa, and Asia
Leatherback turtles	*Dermochelys coriacea*	Oceanic Islands, Atlantic Ocean, Pacific Ocean, Indian Ocean, Mediterranean Sea
File snake	*Acrochordus arafurae*	Northern Australia, New Guinea

Glossary

algae—small plants without roots or stems that grow in water or damp places

carapace—the top part of a turtle's shell

chorion—a membrane surrounding an embryo that provides it with oxygen

class—a group of creatures that share certain characteristics. Turtles, snakes, lizards, tuatara, alligators, and crocodiles are all in the same class—the reptiles.

cold-blooded—the term for an animal whose body temperature depends on environment

egg tooth—a hard point on a hatching animal's snout or beak that helps it break out of the shell

embryo—an unborn or unhatched animal in an early stage of development

evolve—to change slowly over generations, developing specialized physical characteristics or behaviors

incubation period—the time it takes for a newly laid egg to hatch

kingdom—the top-level category for classifying living things. The five kingdoms are plants, animals, protists, fungi, and bacteria.

parthenogenesis—reproduction by females without mating with a male

pelvis—the hipbones

pheromone—a scent that some animals produce that attracts a mate

placenta—a structure with many blood vessels in the uterus of most mammals and a few other animals that nourishes the embryo

plastron—the bottom part of a turtle's shell

scutes—the horny scales on a turtle's shell

taxonomy—the science of organizing living things into categories

venomous—able to inject poison into another animal

vertebrate—an animal that has a backbone

yolk sac—a food-rich sac inside an egg that nourishes the embryo

To Find Out More

Books

Coborn, John. *Lizards.* Broomall, PA: Chelsea House, 1998.

Julivert, Maria Angels. *The Fascinating World of Snakes.* Hauppauge, NY: Barrons Juveniles, 1993.

Ling, Mary, et al. *Snake Book.* New York: DK Publishing, 1997.

Lovett, Sarah. *Extremely Weird Snakes.* Santa Fe, NM: John Muir Publications, 1996.

Pipe, Jim. *Giant Book of Snakes and Slithery Creatures.* Brookfield, CT: Copper Beach, 1998.

Stotsky, Sandra. *Let's Hear It for Herps!: All About Reptiles and Amphibians.* Broomall, PA: Chelsea House, 1998.

Organizations and Online Sites

Lizards! A Live Expedition with the American Museum of Natural History
http://www.discovery.com/exp/lizards/lizards.html
This site follows a team of lizard researchers on a desert expedition. Movies, sounds, and many pictures are included.

Nature Explorer: World of Reptiles
http://www.natureexplorer.com/WR/WR.html
This site discusses how reptiles are related to other animals, as well as providing specific information about individual reptiles.

NOVA Online: Crocodiles
http://www.pbs.org/wgbh/nova/crocs/
A companion to a public television show, this site is the ultimate guide to crocodilians, with everything from their survival strategies to the basics on all 23 species of crocodiles to what it's like to wrestle with a half-ton Nile crocodile in the wild.

Reptiles Magazine
http://www.animalnetwork.com/reptiles/default.asp
This site contains answers to frequently-asked questions about reptiles, a calendar of reptile-related events, and more.

Society for the Study of Amphibians and Reptiles
http://www.ukans.edu/~ssar/
This organization's web site provides information about reptile conservation and careers studying reptiles.

U.S. Fish and Wildlife Service
http://www.fws.gov
This United States government agency has information on endangered species, habitat conservation, and more.

World-Wide Kids Network—Reptiles and Amphibians
http://www.worldkids.com/critter/reptiles/wel/
This site provides information on these animals and a "critters contest" as well.

Yahooligans
http://www.yahooligans.com/Science_and_Nature/
Living_Things/Reptiles_and_Amphibians/
This site is a directory of information on all kinds of reptiles and amphibians.

A Note on Sources

The first thing I did when I began this book was to sift through my memories. Over the years, I have taken numerous courses in natural history and visited dozens of zoos, aquariums, and nature preserves around the world. Thinking about those experiences gave me ideas for strange reptiles to include. My next step was to browse through my personal nature library for ideas and facts. Palmer and Fowler's *Handbook of Natural History*, even though it is old-fashioned and incomplete, gave me leads about various species to research further. *The Encyclopedia of Reptiles & Amphibians* is an excellent reference book that provides an in-depth understanding of the various families and species. Simon and Schuster's guide to *Reptiles and Amphibians of the World* is a handy field guide with pictures and brief descriptions.

I supplemented these books with a few from the local libraries, including children's books.

Finally, once I knew which species I wanted to include, I went to the Internet. By searching for a specific genus and species, I often found some useful information, particularly in sites posted by universities and zoos.

The help of expert consultant Kathy Carlstead, Ph.D., of the Honolulu Zoo in Honolulu, Hawaii, was invaluable in creating this book.

—*Sara Swan Miller*

Index

Numbers in *italics* indicate illustrations.

About the Author

Sara Swan Miller has enjoyed working with children all her life, first as a Montessori nursery school teacher, and later as an outdoor environmental educator at the Mohonk Preserve in New Paltz, New York. As director of the school program at the preserve, she has taught hundreds of children the importance of appreciating and respecting the natural world.

She has written over thirty books, including *Three Stories You Can Read to Your Dog*; *Three Stories You Can Read to Your Cat*; *Three More Stories You Can Read to Your Dog*; and *What's in the Woods?: An Outdoor Activity Book*, as well as four other books on strange animals for the Watts Library.

She has also written several books on farm animals for Children's Press's *True Books* series, and many books on animals for Franklin Watts' *Animals in Order* series, including ones on true bugs, flies, rodents, perching birds, turtles, and salamanders.